STRINGSTASTIC
Level 2
VIOLA

By Lorraine Chai

2nd Edition

STRINGSTASTIC

PO BOX 815 Epping NSW 1710 Australia
www.stringstastic.com
Copyright © 2018 Lorraine Chai
First Published 2018
2nd Edition 2020
American Edition 2021

Book design by Meilisa Lengkong

All rights reserved.
Reproduction in whole or in part for any use whatsoever is strictly prohibited.

THE AUTHOR
LORRAINE CHAI

Lorraine is a multi talented instrumentalist and an international educator. She graduated from the Sydney Conservatorium of Music with a Bachelor of Music Studies in 2008 and completed her Graduate Diploma of Education at the Australian Catholic University a year later.

Having grown up with a musical family, Lorraine began piano lessons at the age of four and violin at the age of six, giving her first violin performance at just seven years of age. Lorraine started teaching violin at the age of 14 and founded a string ensemble at her local church. From there, teaching and performing became her passion.

Lorraine loves finding new and exciting ways students can learn their instrument in a classroom setting as well as in private lessons. Along her musical journey and exposure to the various educational methods including Kodaly, Suzuki, Orff, and Dalcroze, Lorraine has also attended Alexander Technique workshops, and has found that she can integrate these various methods into her own teaching technique for the benefit of her students.

Lorraine has extensive ensemble and orchestral experience in Malaysia and in Australia. Lorraine currently the Music Director of Stringstastic Pty Ltd and is an active member with the Australian Strings Association, AUSTA NSW. She also co-ordinates instrumental programmes and runs string ensembles for some of Sydney's most celebrated schools.

PREFACE

Stringstastic viola Level 2 follows on from the knowledge which young players have gained in Stringstastic viola Level 1. Stringstastic viola Level 2 extends that knowledge through games and fun graphics to assist young beginner violists to help them better understand the instrument and to learn music theory in an enjoyable way. This Stringstastic series can be used in a private lesson or along side the violin and cello book series in a classroom setting.

For extra resources, go to www.stringstastic.com to download them for free.

Have fun!!

ACKNOWLEDGEMENT

This book was made possible with the encouragement of my family and loved ones. I would like to thank the following for their advice and input in making this book possible.

Dr. Rita Crews OAM, FMusA (honoris causa), PhD(UNE), BA(Hons), AMusTCL, GradCertDistEd (UNE), FMusicolASMC, HonFNMSM, DipMus (honoris causa) (AICM) MIMT, MACE, MMTA, JP.

Dr. Anthony Clarke DMA, MMus, Grad Dip, BMus Ed, DSCM, FTCL, LMusA, AMusA

Helen Tuckey PG Dip Music (Manhattan School of Music), AMusA, MIMT, DipArts(music) (Victorian College of the Arts)

CONTENTS

- 4   REVISION
- 6   TEMPO
- 8   QUAVER NOTE AND REST
- 10   4TH FINGER
- 12   DYNAMICS
- 14   SLUR VS. TIE
- 16   WHAT HAVE WE LEARNT SO FAR?
- 19   NOTE MOVEMENT
- 21   LOWERED 2ND FINGER
- 24   TONE AND SEMITONE
- 29   REVISION - NOTE READING ON ALL STRINGS
- 31   SCALES AND ARPEGGIOS
- 38   KEY SIGNATURE VS. ACCIDENTAL
- 40   ARTICULATION
- 42   SIGNS
- 44   LAST REVISION
- 47   TEST

STRINGSTASTIC

Revision

1. Name the 4 open strings of the viola.

   _____
   _____
   _____
   _____

2. Fill in the blanks.

NOTE	NOTE NAME	REST	REST NAME	VALUE
♩			Crotchet rest	
		𝄽		2
	Semibreve			4

3. In semibreves, draw and name the notes of each string of the viola. (Don't forget the ♯s).

   C String

   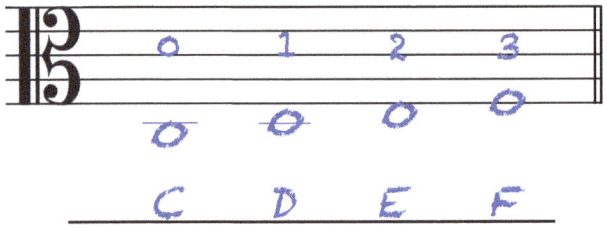

   D String

   G String

   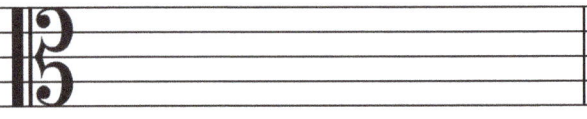

   A String

   _____

4. Put in the bar lines and write in the beats.

5. Name the missing notes of these fingerings on the fingerboard.

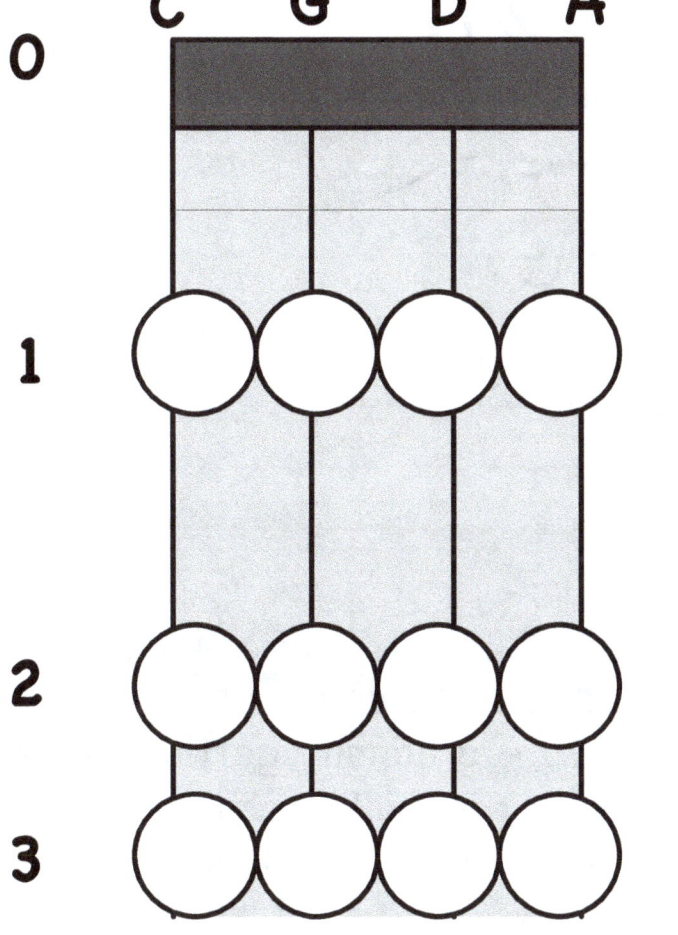

Tempo

Tempo is the speed at which music is played.

accelerando (accel.) – gradually getting faster
rallentando (rall.) – gradually getting slower
ritardando (rit.) – gradually getting slower
a tempo – return to original speed

Match each picture to its meaning.

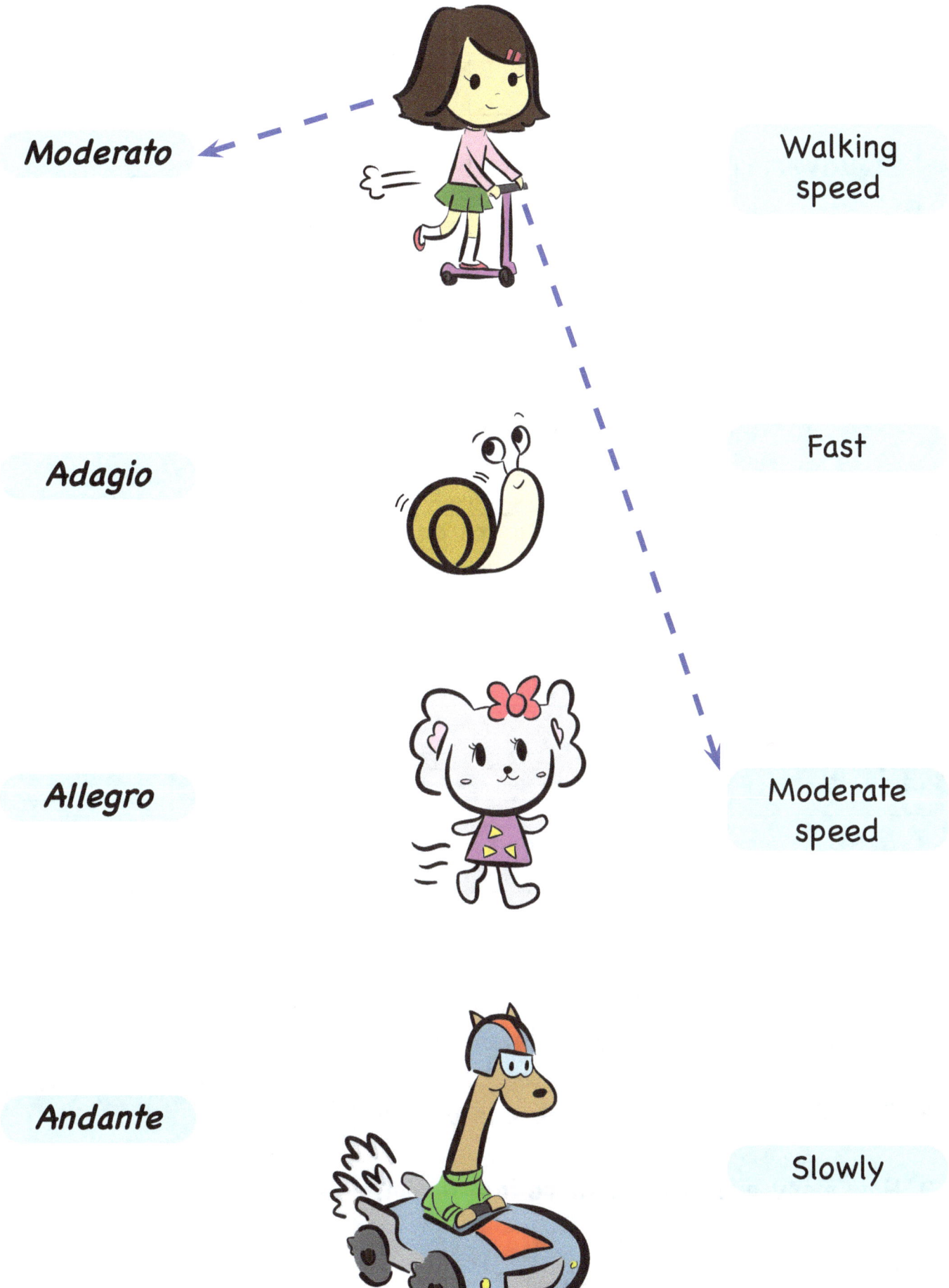

Quaver Note and Rest

NAME	NOTE	REST	VALUE
Quaver	♪ ←tail	tail→ 𝄾	½
2 Quavers joined	♫ ←beam = ♩		½ + ½ = 1

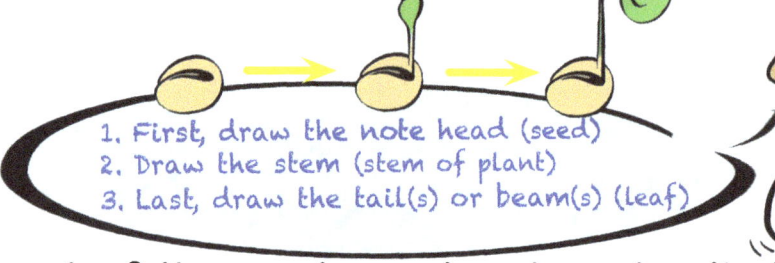

1. First, draw the note head (seed)
2. Draw the stem (stem of plant)
3. Last, draw the tail(s) or beam(s) (leaf)

Draw the tail for each of these notes and rests and write its value.

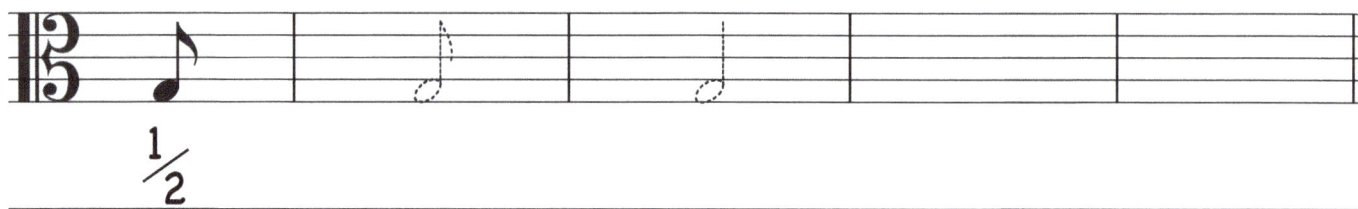

½

½

Answer the questions below.

1. How many minims are there in a semibreve?

2. How many crotchets are there in a minim?

3. How many quavers are there in a minim?

4. A 𝅝 is equal to ___ ♪ s

5. A 𝄻 is equal to ___ 𝄾 s

Tommy forgot to close the cover to his collection of bugs and now they are all over the living room. He has to get them back into their appropriate boxes before his mother comes home. Colour the bugs according to the number of counts.

COUNTS	COLOUR
1	RED
2	BLUE
3	GREEN
4	YELLOW

How many bugs are there in the following?

Red   -   bugs

Blue   -   bugs

Green -   bugs

Yellow -   bugs

4th Finger

Your 4th finger is often used to match the pitch of the next higher open string.

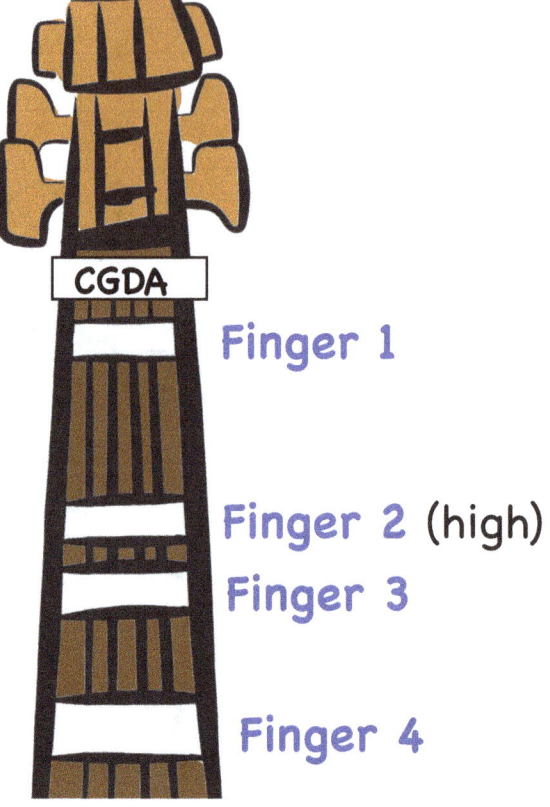

CGDA

Finger 1

Finger 2 (high)
Finger 3

Finger 4

We use the 4th finger to create a smoother sound or fewer changes between strings to help with bowing.

Try playing these notes with the indicated fingering.

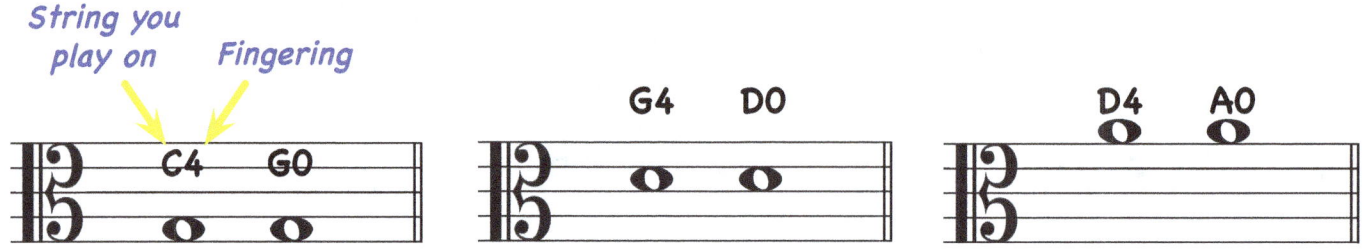

String you play on *Fingering*

Do they sound the same?
Play these notes for your mum and dad and see if they can tell if you were playing on an open string or using the 4th finger.

Could they hear the difference?

Play each of these short tunes.

Although some notes work better playing using the open string, circle the notes which you could also play with your 4th finger.

Dynamics

Dynamics refers to the volume of a sound or note.

Which animal makes a LOUD or soft sound?

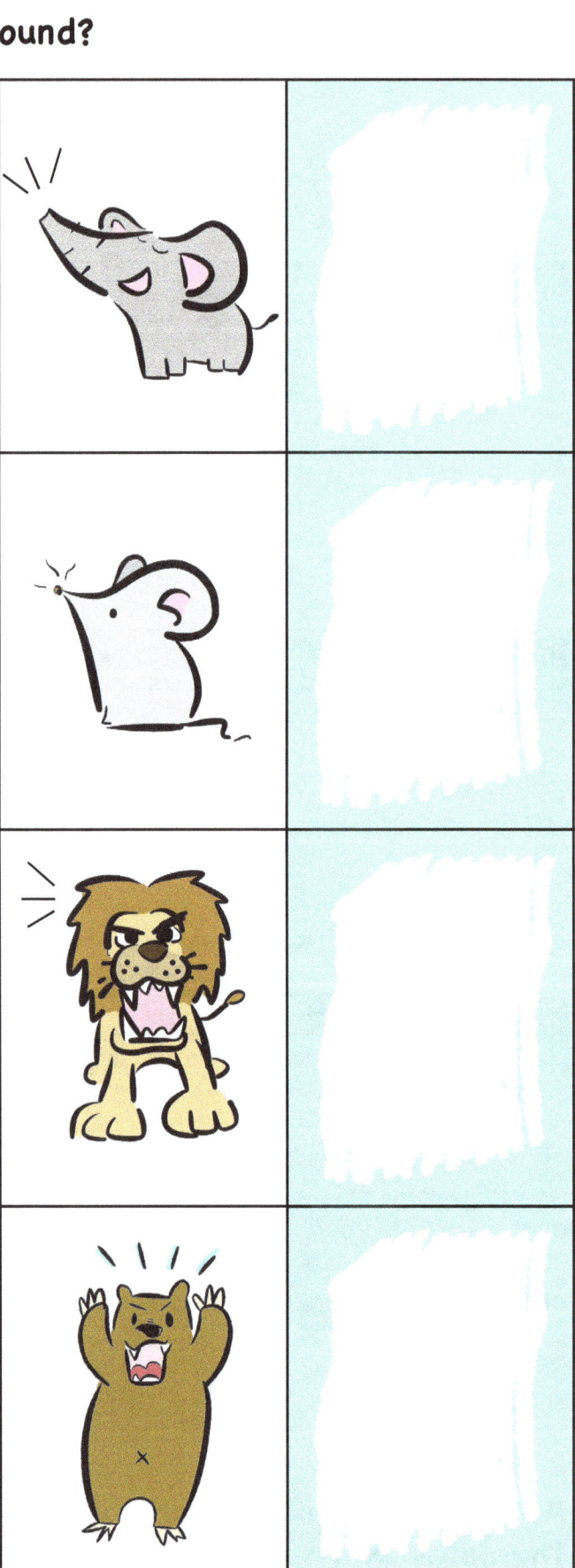

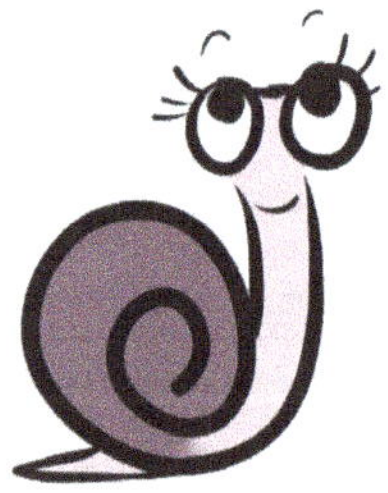	soft p		
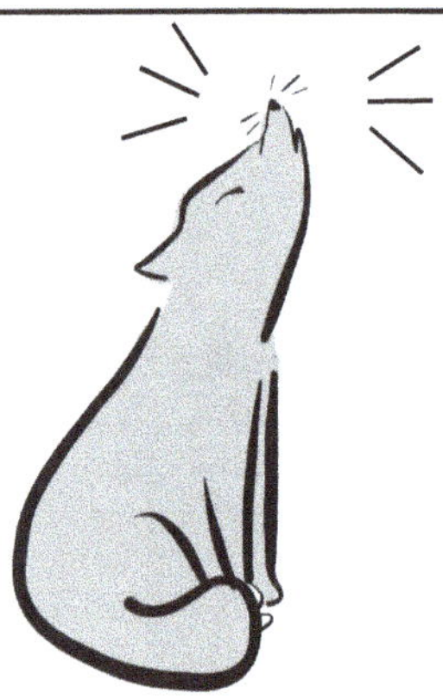			
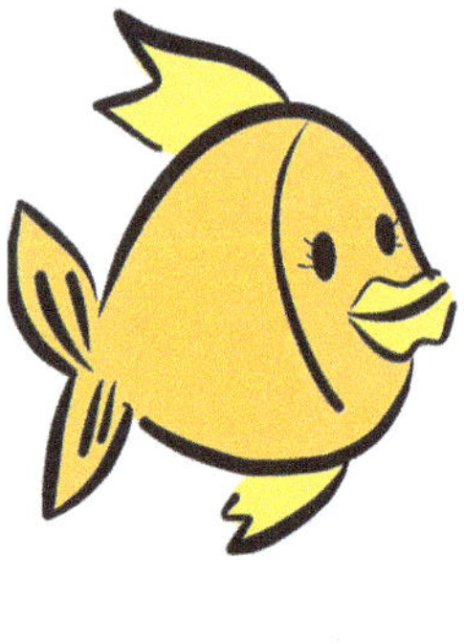			
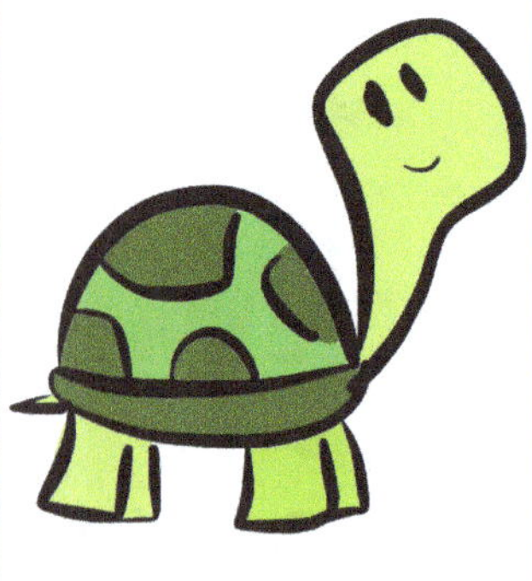			

We use Italian terms to express dynamics. Below are the meanings of each Italian term.

forte (f) - LOUD
piano (p) - soft
crescendo (cresc.) - ⟨ - gradually getting louder
decrescendo (decresc.) - ⟩ - gradually getting softer
diminuendo (dim.) - gradually getting softer

mezzo (m) - moderately (medium)
mezzo piano (mp) - moderately (medium) soft
mezzo forte (mf) - moderately (medium) loud

Fill in the blank below arranging each dynamic starting from the softest to the loudest.

⟨ *mp* ⟨ ⟨ *f*

On the previous page, mark out the volume each animal makes by using *p* for *piano* or *f* for *forte*.

Guess what?

Play similar notes in a row on your violin using different dynamics each time. (*f, p, cresc., dim.*).

You can play this game with your friends. Ask them if they can guess what kind of dynamic you are playing.

Slur vs. Tie

Slurs and ties are curved lines joining 2 or more notes. They look the same however their function varies.

SLUR	TIE
♪♪♪ ← slur	♪♪ ← tie
Notes sound and played _smoothly_	_Hold_ the note at the total amount of notes
Keep bow moving in the same direction while changing your fingers	Keep bow moving in the same direction
Joined between _different_ notes	Joined between 2 of the _same_ notes

How long do you hold these tied notes for?

♩ ♩ = 1 + 1 = 2

♩ 𝅗𝅥 = =

♩ ♩ ♩ = =

♩ ♪ = =

𝅗𝅥 𝅗𝅥 = =

Information: The Italian term for playing smoothly is legato

Identify if these curved lines are either a tie or slur.

slur

What have we learnt so far?

What does "*Allegro*" mean?

What does "*Andante*" mean?

What does "*a tempo*" mean?

What is the total beats of all these rest and notes?

Fill in the blanks.

𝅗𝅥.	dotted minim	mp	
	gradually getting softer		LOUD
rit.		cresc.	
♪		(two notes on staff)	slur
(two slurred notes on staff)			quaver rest
	minim rest		gradually getting faster

Match each picture to its meaning.

Adagio   f

p   Allegro   accel.

Between 2 notes, circle one in which you can use both the open string and the 4th finger.

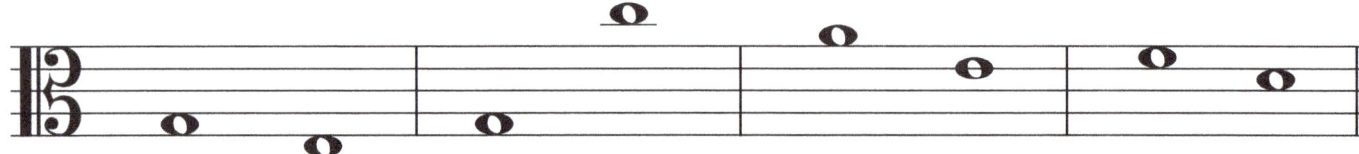

How many crotchet beats are these notes and rests?

♩ = *1*   𝄽 =

♪ =   𝅗𝅥 =

𝅗𝅥. =   𝄽 =

𝄾 =   ♫ =

𝄻 =   𝅝 =

Note Movement

Notice how notes move up or down in the stave. Be aware of how far the notes move (through a line or in a space).

STEP	space-line line-space	add a finger or take one away
SKIP	space-space line-line	skip a finger upwards or downwards

Circle the 2 notes moving by step.

20
Where should these notes be?

Name the movement of these notes.

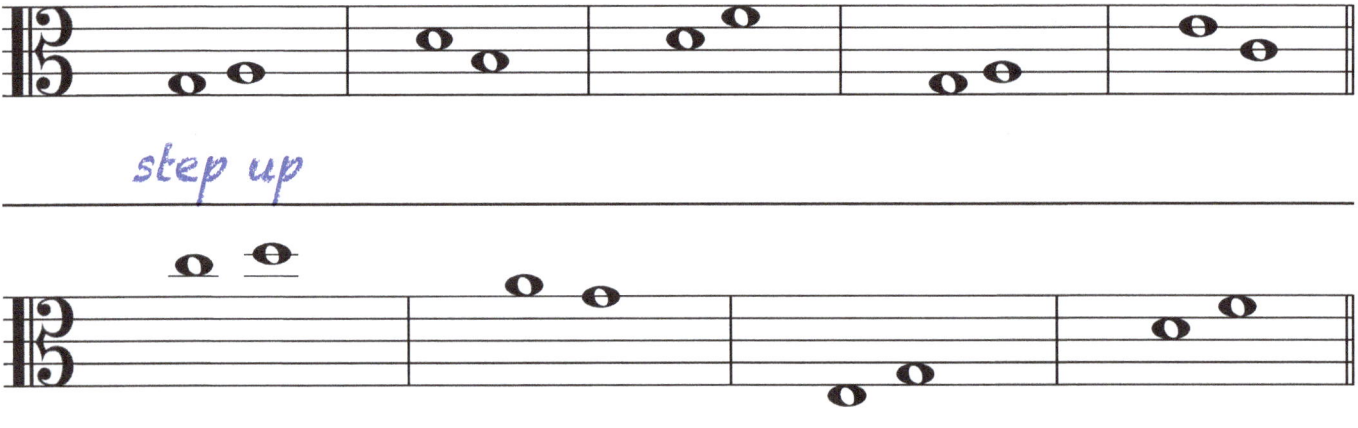

step up

Lowered 2nd Finger

Let us revise the accidentals and our notes on the viola following where the white strips are placed.

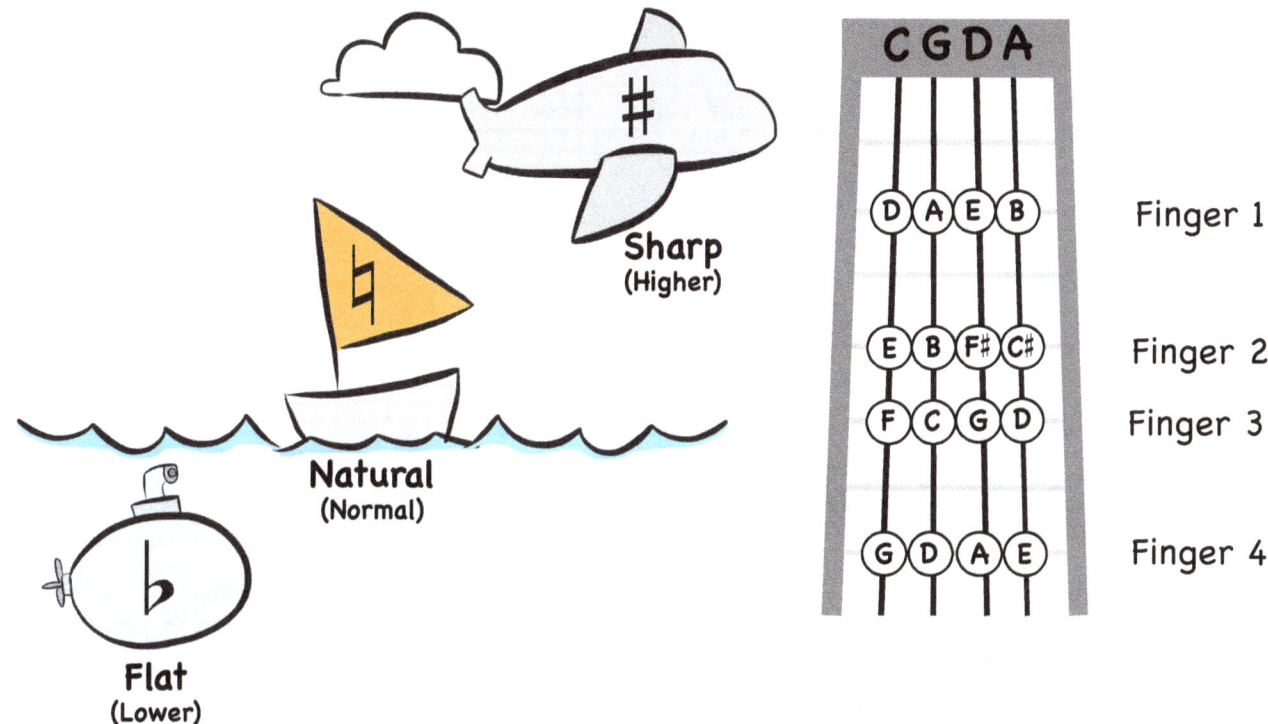

The pitch of the note is lowered when the 2nd finger is placed lower away from the 3rd finger (next to 1st finger).

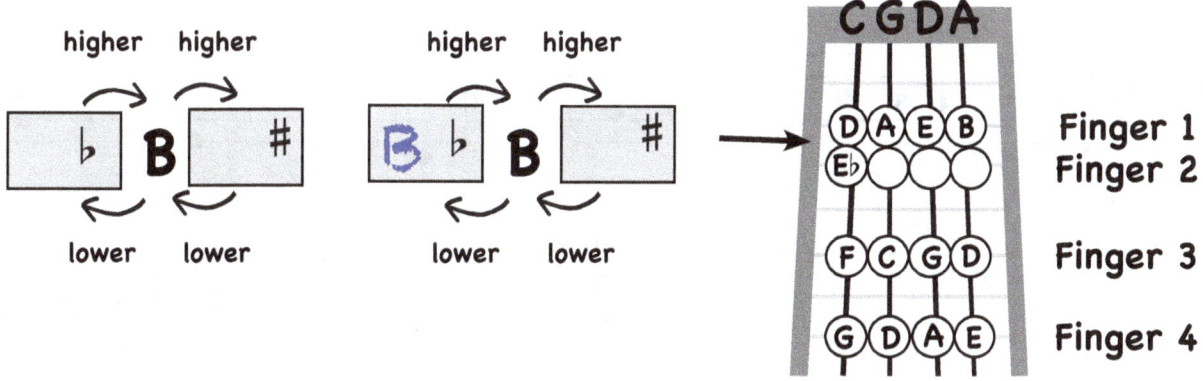

Name the other lowered 2nd finger.

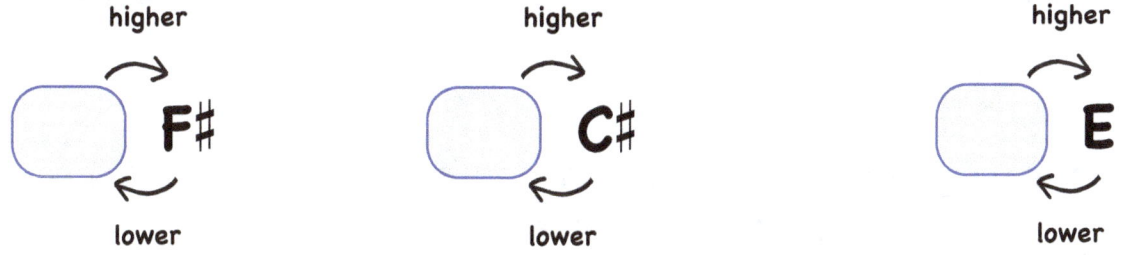

22

Circle the notes where you use the 2nd finger and mark them with arrows on top of the note.

↓ - 2nd finger next to the 1st finger

↑ - 2nd finger on the line next to the 3rd finger

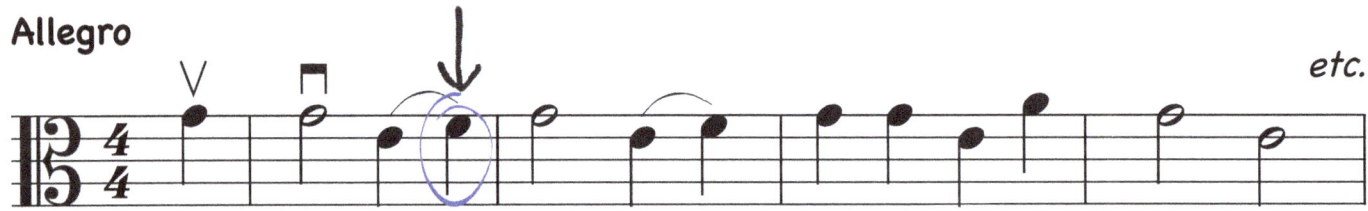

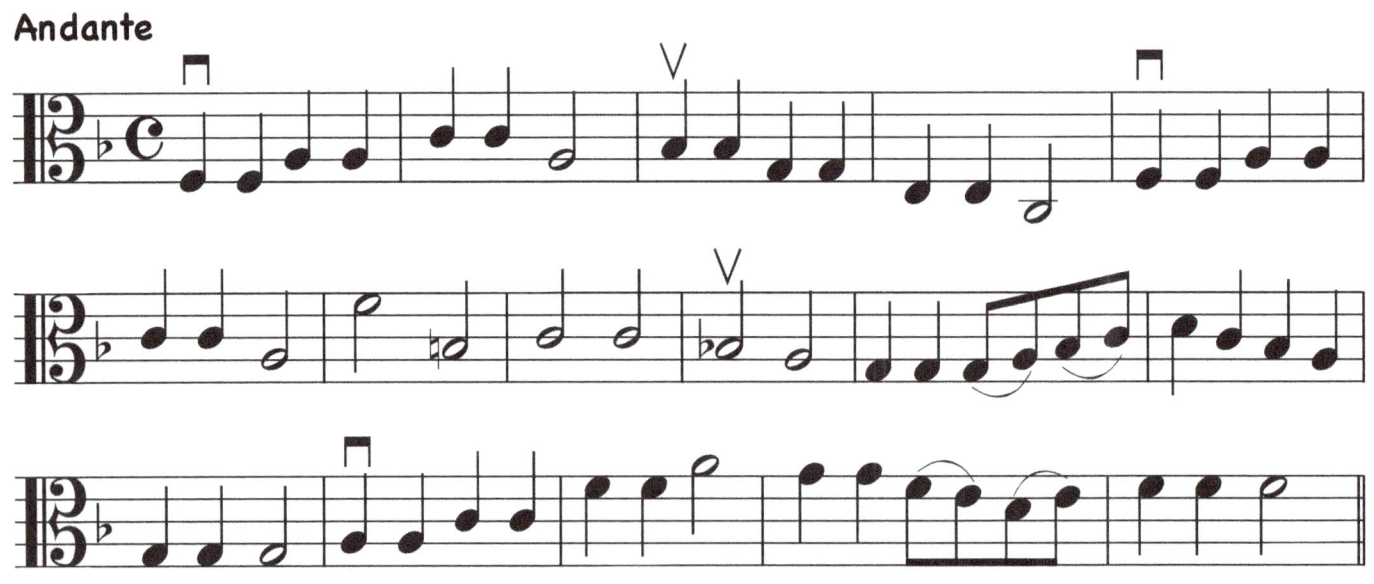

Play these short tunes. You can perform a small concert to your family with these songs.

Lower each note and name them.
(You do not have to place a natural sign after the letter. Only before the note.)

F#   F♮   E   C#   B

Raise each note and name them.

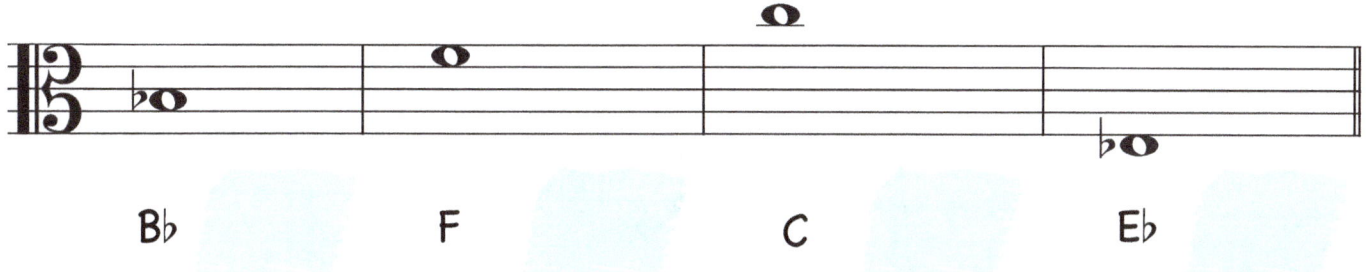

B♭   F   C   E♭

Draw the notes below as indicated. (Remember your ♮.)

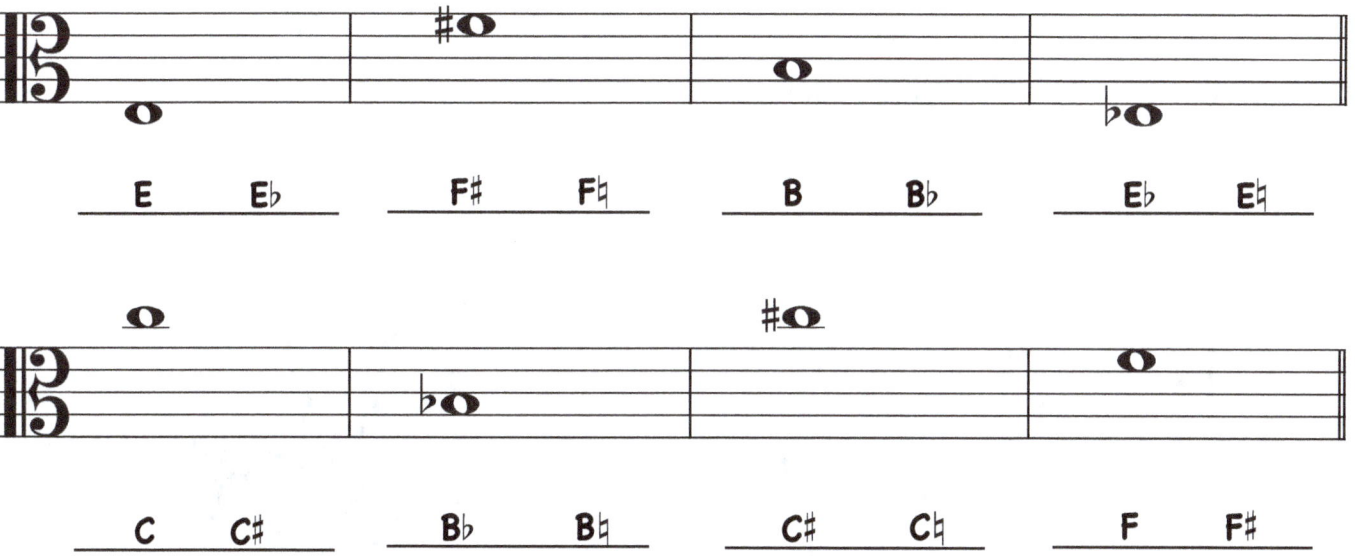

E   E♭   F#   F♮   B   B♭   E♭   E♮

C   C#   B♭   B♮   C#   C♮   F   F#

Now add an arrow on the 2nd note pointing down (↓) or up (↑) indicating if the 2nd finger note is lowered or raised.

Tone and Semitone

A **Semitone** (half step) is the smallest distance between 2 notes.
When you play semitone on the viola, your fingers would be placed right **next to each other** on the fingerboard.

Let us revise our notes on the viola.

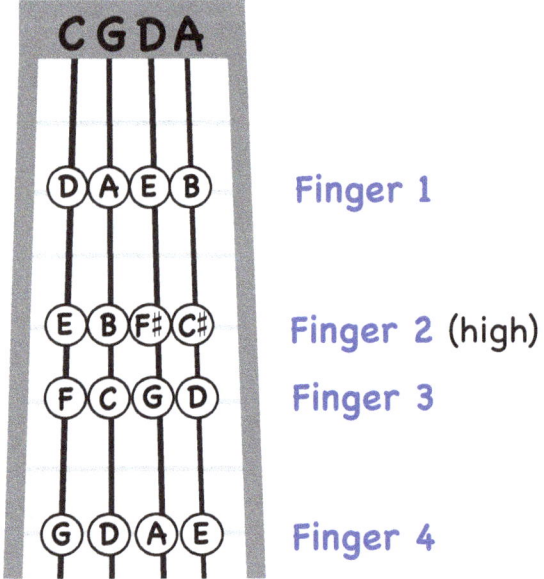

And a quick revision of your accidentals...

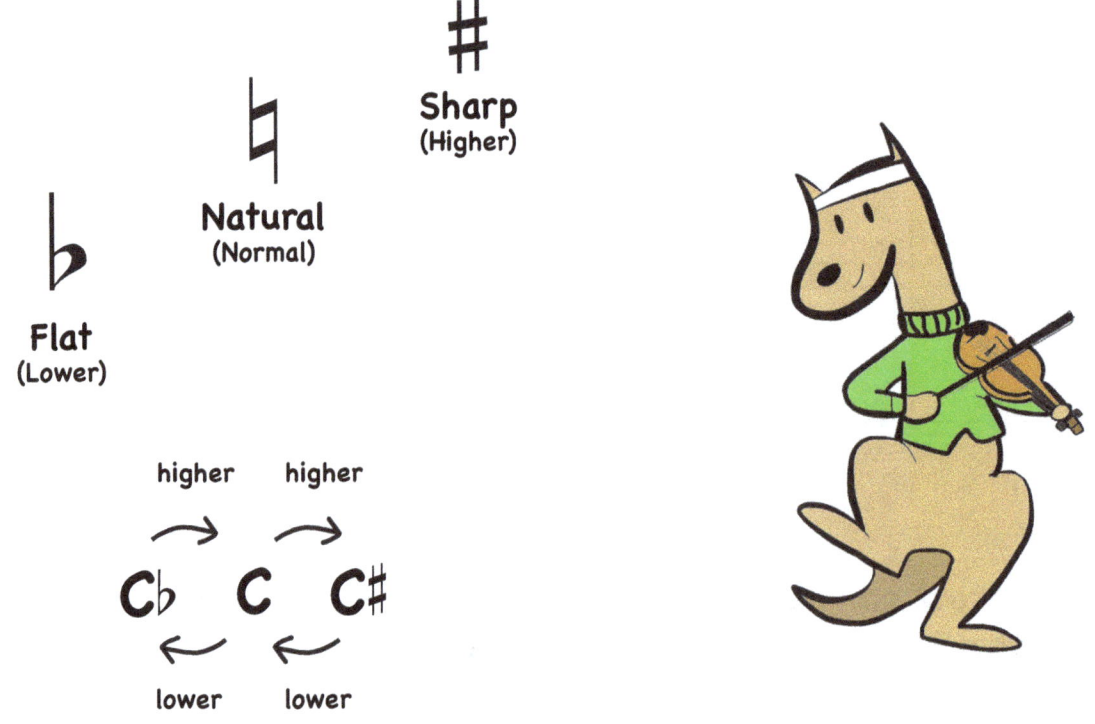

Insert the correct notes.

1.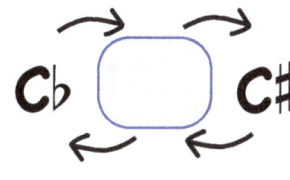

2.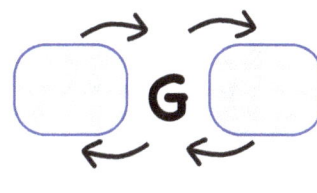

3.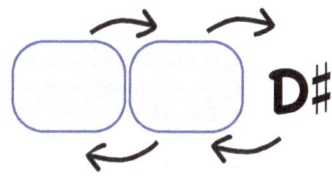

4.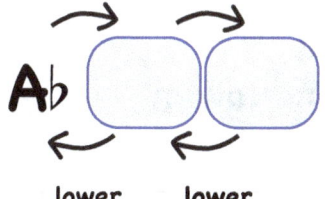

5.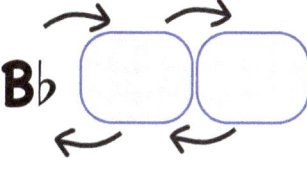

6.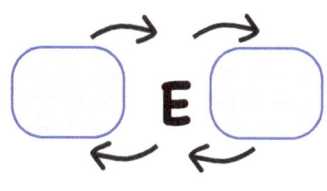

7.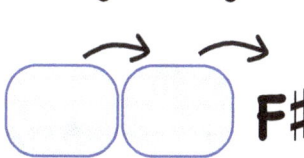

26

Let us look at semitones on the viola fingerboard.
Circle 4 pairs of notes which are a semitone apart.

Information:
Enharmonic means TWO different note names that sound the same.
eg. E# = F

TIP: Name the first note and then visualize the notes on the fingerboard.

After each note, draw a note that is a semitone higher.

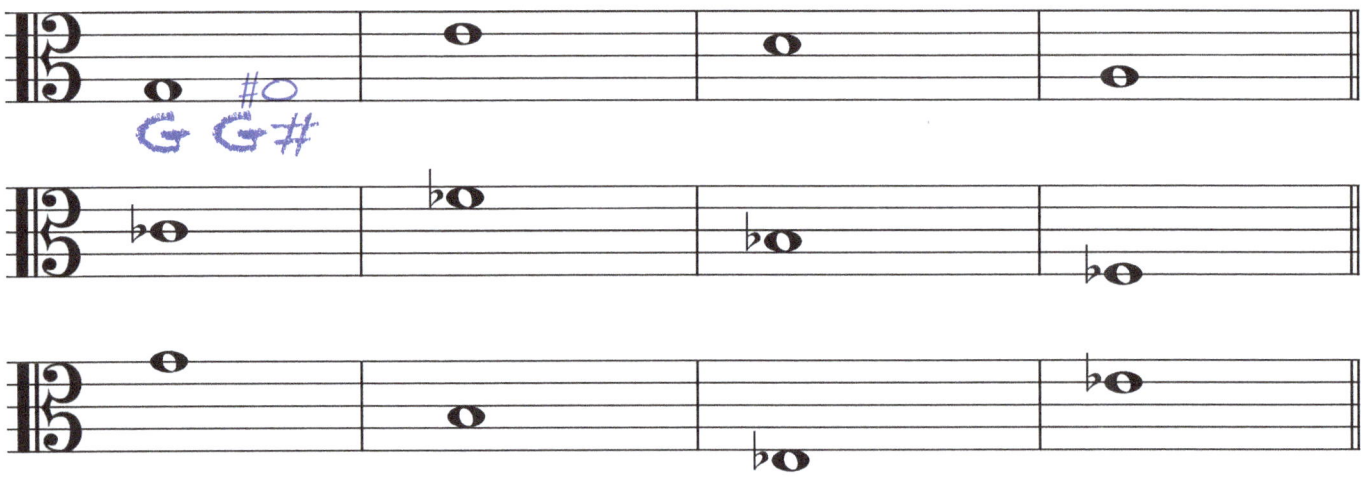

G   G#

After each note, draw a note that is a semitone lower.

A **Tone** (whole step) means the notes are 2 semitones away from each other.

When you play the viola, 2 of your fingers next to each other have a space between them. So fingers would be placed **away from each other** on the fingerboard.

Circle 12 pairs of notes which are a tone apart.

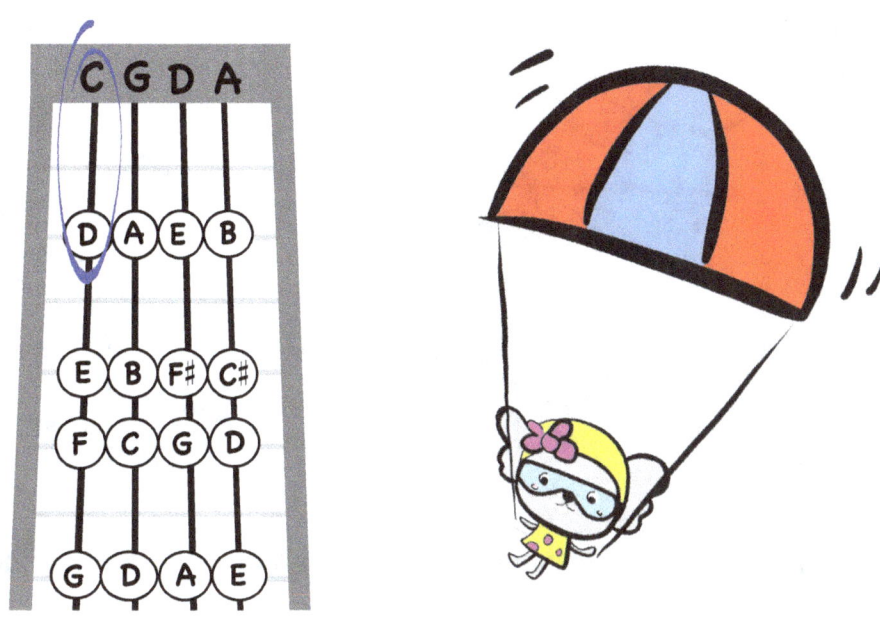

After each note, draw a note that is a tone higher.

After each note, draw a note that is a tone lower.

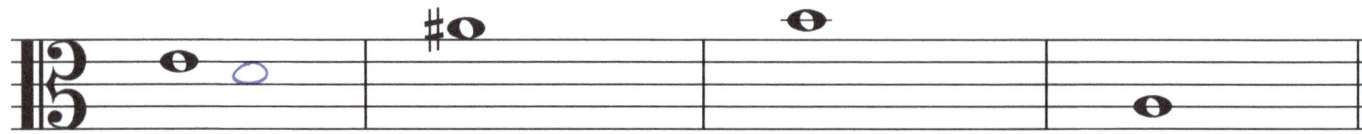

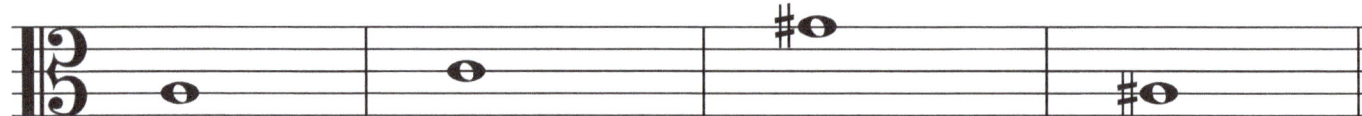

TIP: Name the first note and then visualize the notes on the fingerboard.

Draw the notes according to the steps.

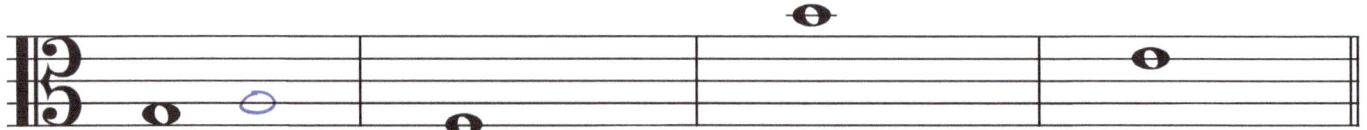

| tone up | semitone up | semitone down | tone down |

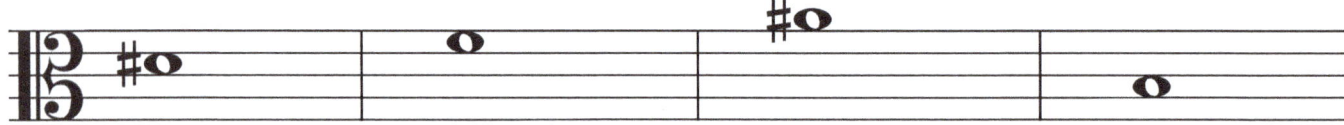

| semitone up | tone up | tone down | tone up |

Revision (Note Reading on all Strings)

In minims, draw and name **all the notes** which can be played on each string. (Don't forget the ♯s.)

Careful of the stem directions

C string
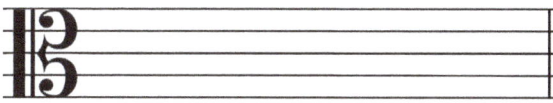

D string
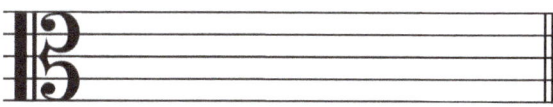

G string
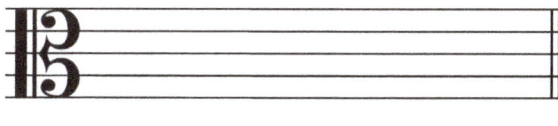

A string
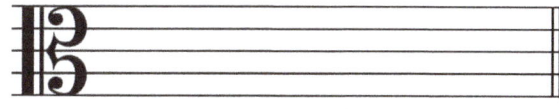

Name the notes.

G

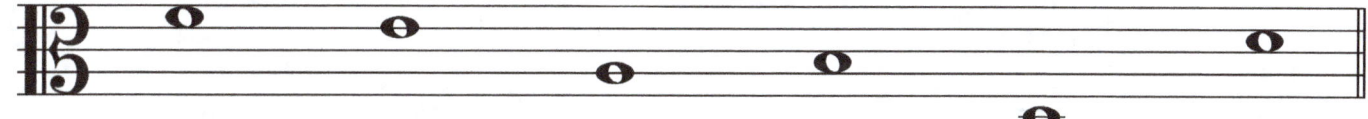

30

Name the notes and put in the bar lines.

C

Match the notes below to the following words.

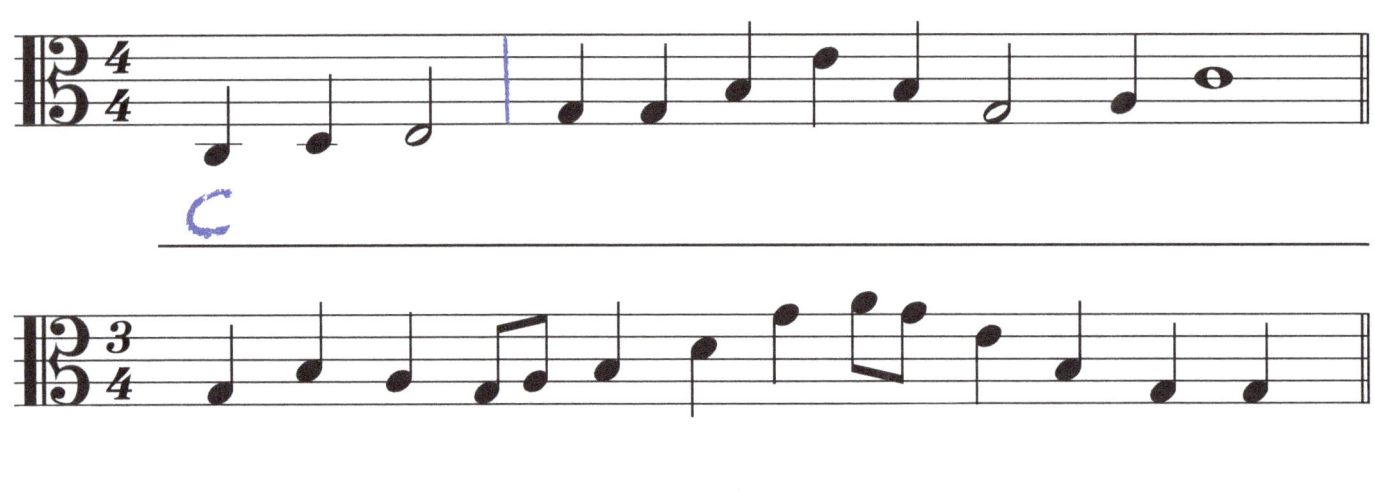

- BED

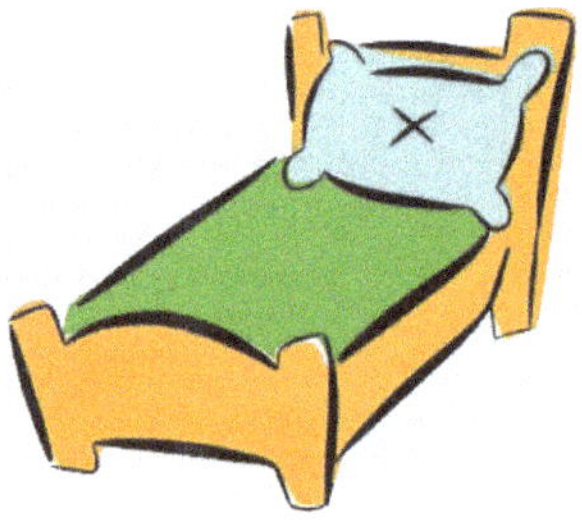

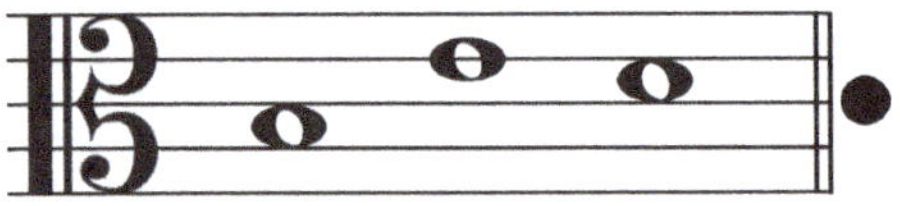

- BAG

- FACE

- CAGE

Scales and Arpeggios

A **Scale** is a musical ladder with notes stepping up and down in alphabetical order starting from the name of the note of the scale to the next note of the same name.

Eg.
C Major (1 octave)

C   D   E   F   G   A   B   C

Octave – is a series of 8 notes (example: A B C D E F G A).

It is the note and the same note higher or lower which includes all the notes in between.

What are the notes for these 2 scales?

G Major (1 octave)
- Remember to add a ♯ on the F as this scale has an F♯.

D Major (1 octave)
- Remember to add ♯s on the F and C notes as this scale has an F♯ and a C♯.

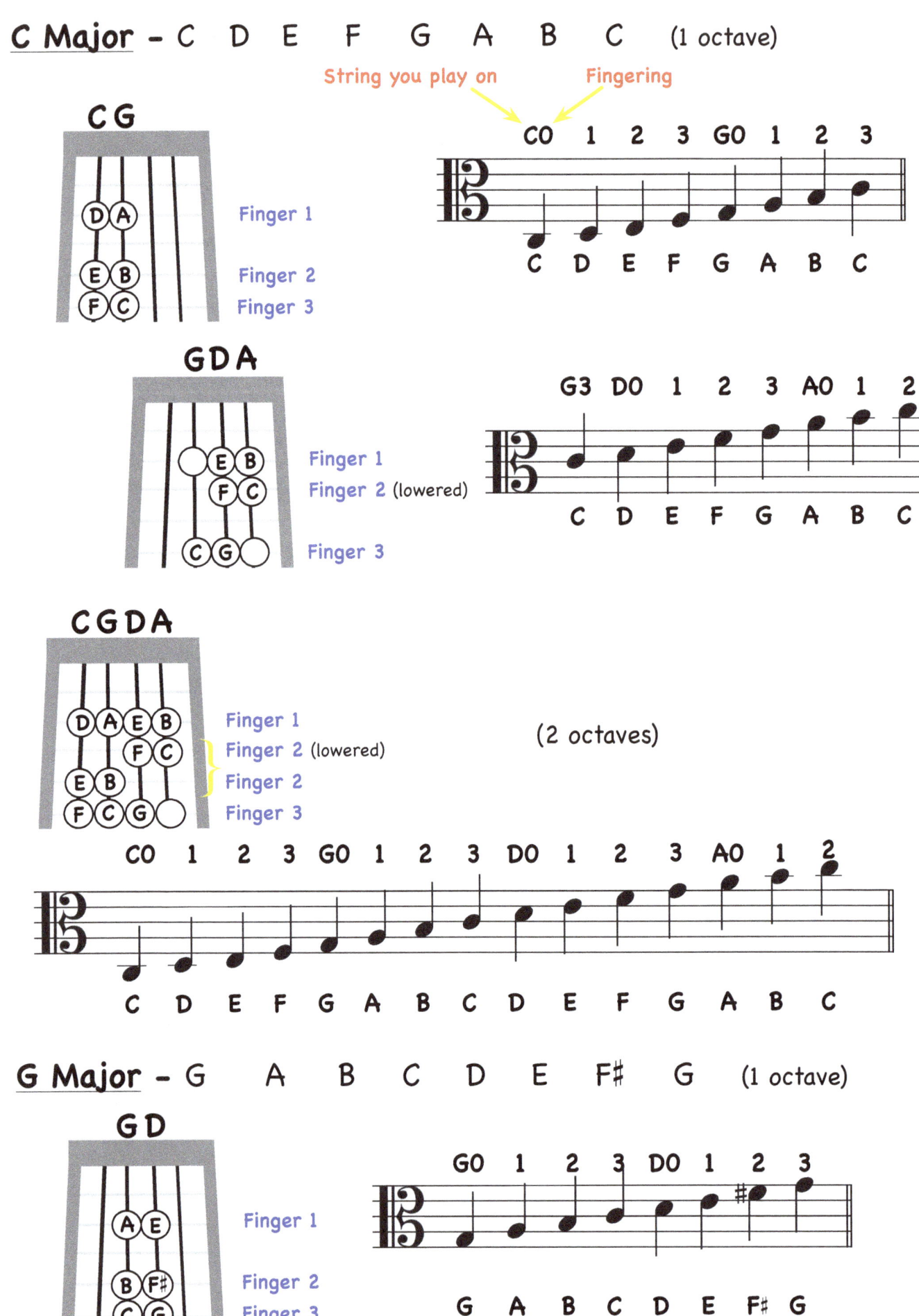

D Major - D E F# G A B C# D   (1 octave)

Now try playing these scales on your viola. Can you play these scales by memory? Let us try...

34 Write in the notes names on the fingerboard and using semibreves, draw the notes of these scales in an ascending (going up) order only.

G major (1 octave)

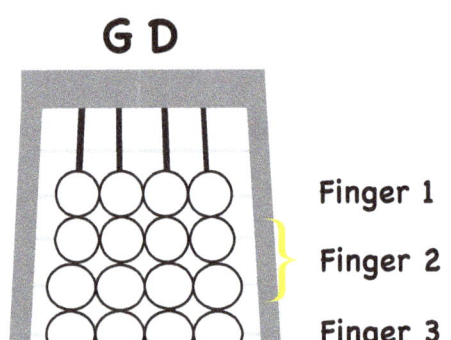
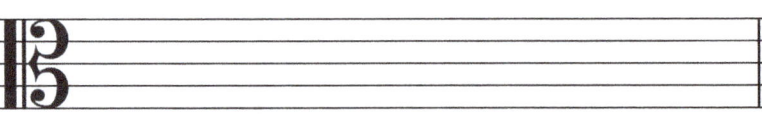

C major (1 octave)

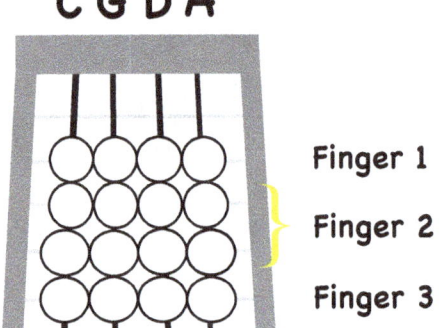

Careful on where the notes should be on the fingerboard.

D major (1 octave)

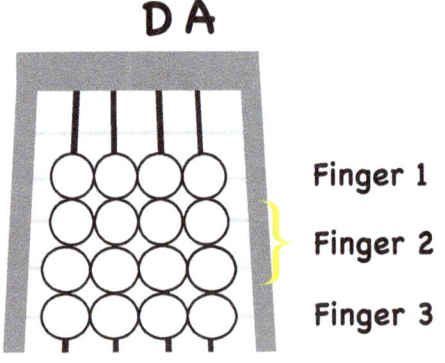
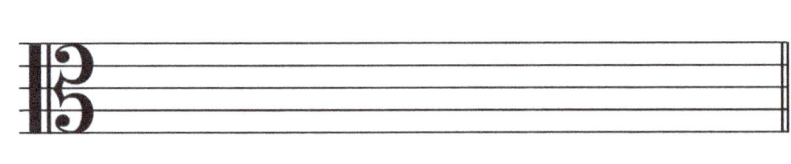

Arpeggios are notes of a chord played one after another. We mainly use the 1st, 3rd and 5th notes of a scale. We also include the 8th note.

Eg.
C Major

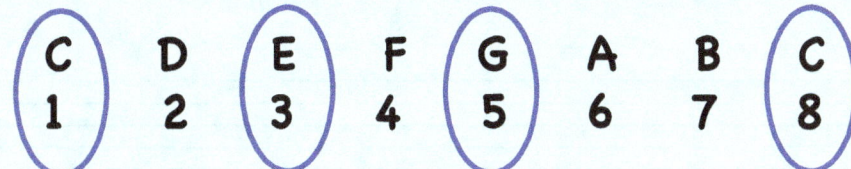

Circle the notes of the arpeggio of the scales below.

G major

        G A B C D E F# G

D major

        D E F# G A B C# D

A chord is two or more notes played together at the same time.

Using minim notes, draw the notes of the arpeggio from these scales in an ascending (going up) **and descending** (going down) **order.**

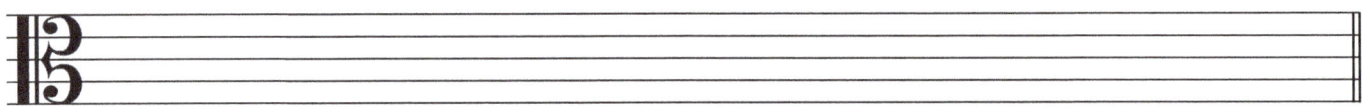

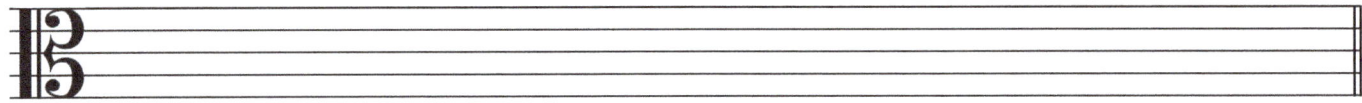

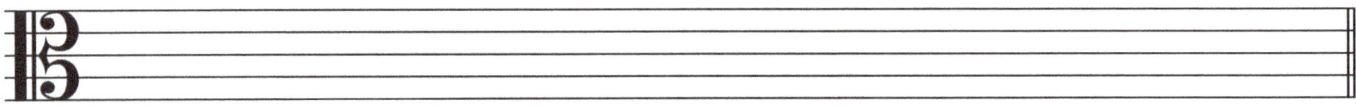

Add the fingering on top of the notes of these arpeggios.

Suzie and Tommy are learning their scales. Help Tommy find his arpeggios and Suzie find her scales.

Key Signature and Accidental

 A **key signature** tells us which notes to play with ♯s and ♭s throughout the piece. These signs are written at the beginning of each line.

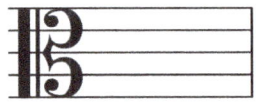
C major
There are no ♯s or ♭s in a C major scale.

G major
There is an F♯ in a G major scale.

D major
There is an F♯ and a C♯ in a D major scale.

Copy the key signature in the next 3 bars.

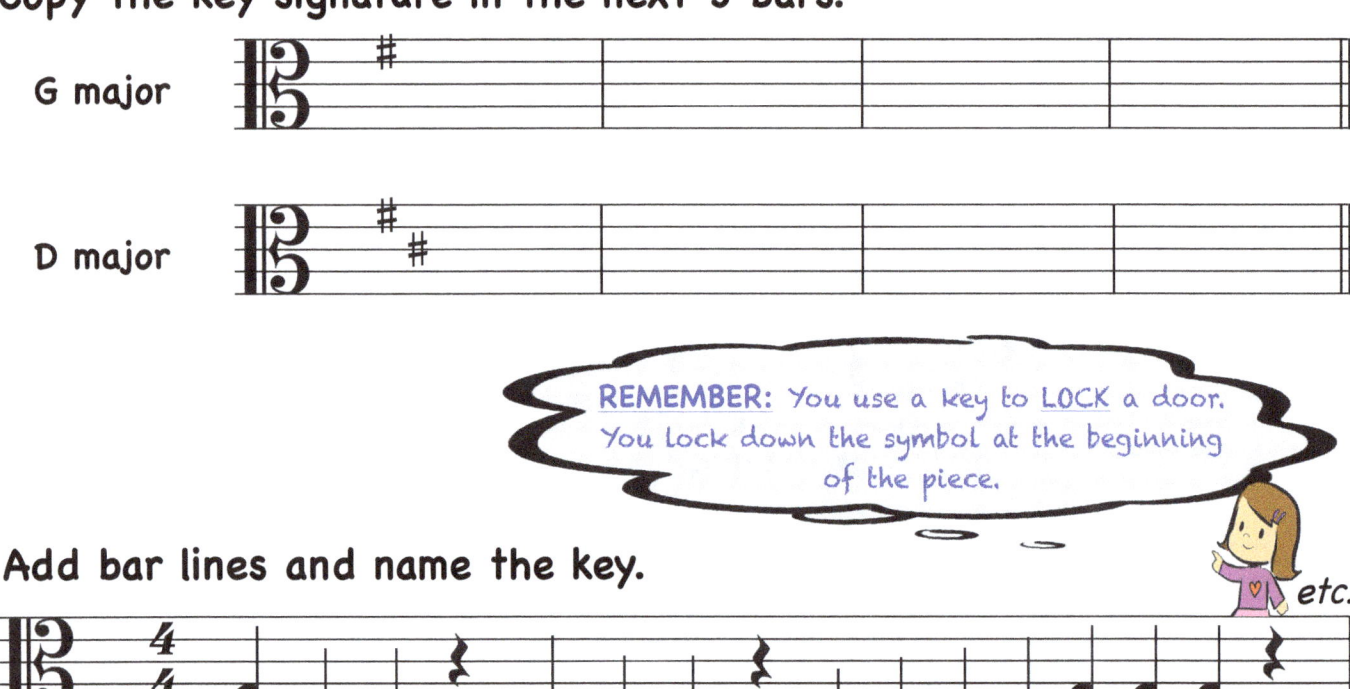

REMEMBER: You use a key to LOCK a door. You lock down the symbol at the beginning of the piece.

Add bar lines and name the key.

Key:

Key:

Key:

Accidentals are signs (♯, ♭, ♮) that are written on the left hand side of a note to change the pitch (how high or low a sound is).

Add the accidentals to the indicated keys and write in the correct time signature.

What is the difference between a key signature and an accidental?

_____

_____

REMEMBER: Think of accidentals as an <u>accident</u> where a symbol is accidentally dropped next to a note.

Articulation

Articulation refers to the different ways of playing the same note creating different sounds.

On stringed instruments, articulation relies on the type of bowing or plucking technique used.

Below are a few articulations which we use as string players.

ARTICULATION	DESCRIPTION
Staccato	Short and detached (bouncy and light)
Accent / Marcato	Strong attack of a note by putting pressure on the bow when playing the note
Tenuto (legato accent)	Slight pressure placed on the bow and held for the full duration of the note
Hooked notes	2 or more notes played in the same direction of the bow with a stop between each note
slur	Playing the notes in one bow direction making the notes sound smooth and connected
pizz. (pizzicato)	Plucking the string of the violin using your finger

Try playing each articulation on one note and using a few notes as a slur. Did you successfully achieve this?

What are these articulations called?

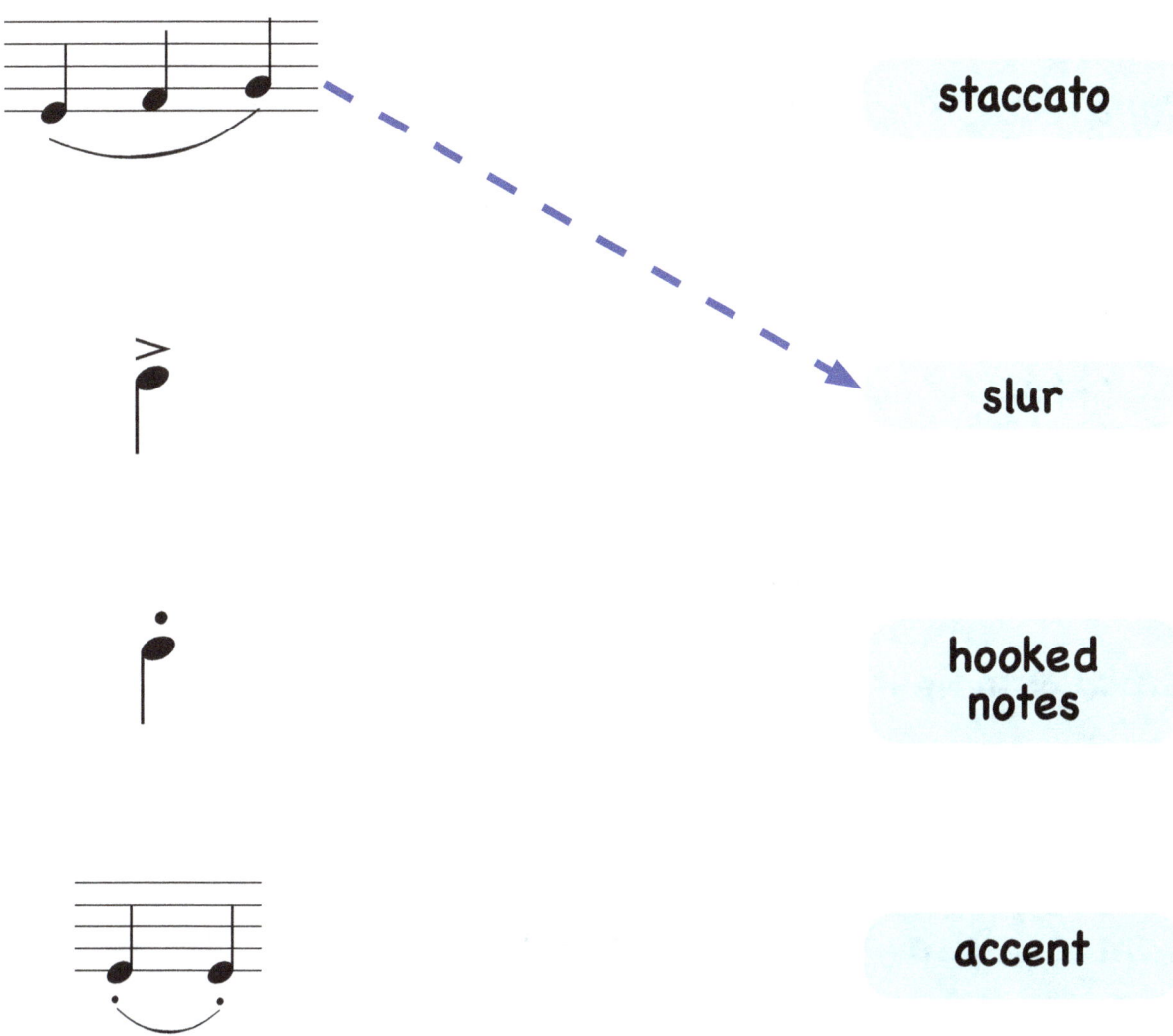

Demonstrate each articulation on the D string.

Now let us see if you can show the same articulation on a different string.

Signs

Da Capo, D.C. – go back to the beginning of the piece

Dal Segno, D.S. – go back to the sign

𝄋 , *segno* – sign

Fine – finish

dolce – sweetly

expressivo – expressively

maestoso – majestically

con spirito – with spirit

fermata / pause – holding the note longer then its value

(Usually hold it twice as long. Think of the pause button on your TV remote control. When you press it, it freezes the video.)

REPEAT SIGNS

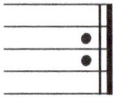 – go back to the beginning and play the music again

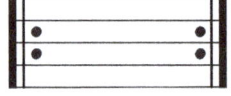 – play this section again

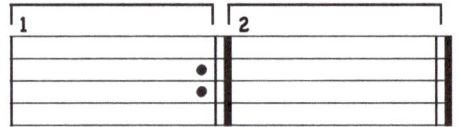 – play the 1st ending the 1st time, skip to 2nd ending on repeat

Match the signs to its correct meaning.

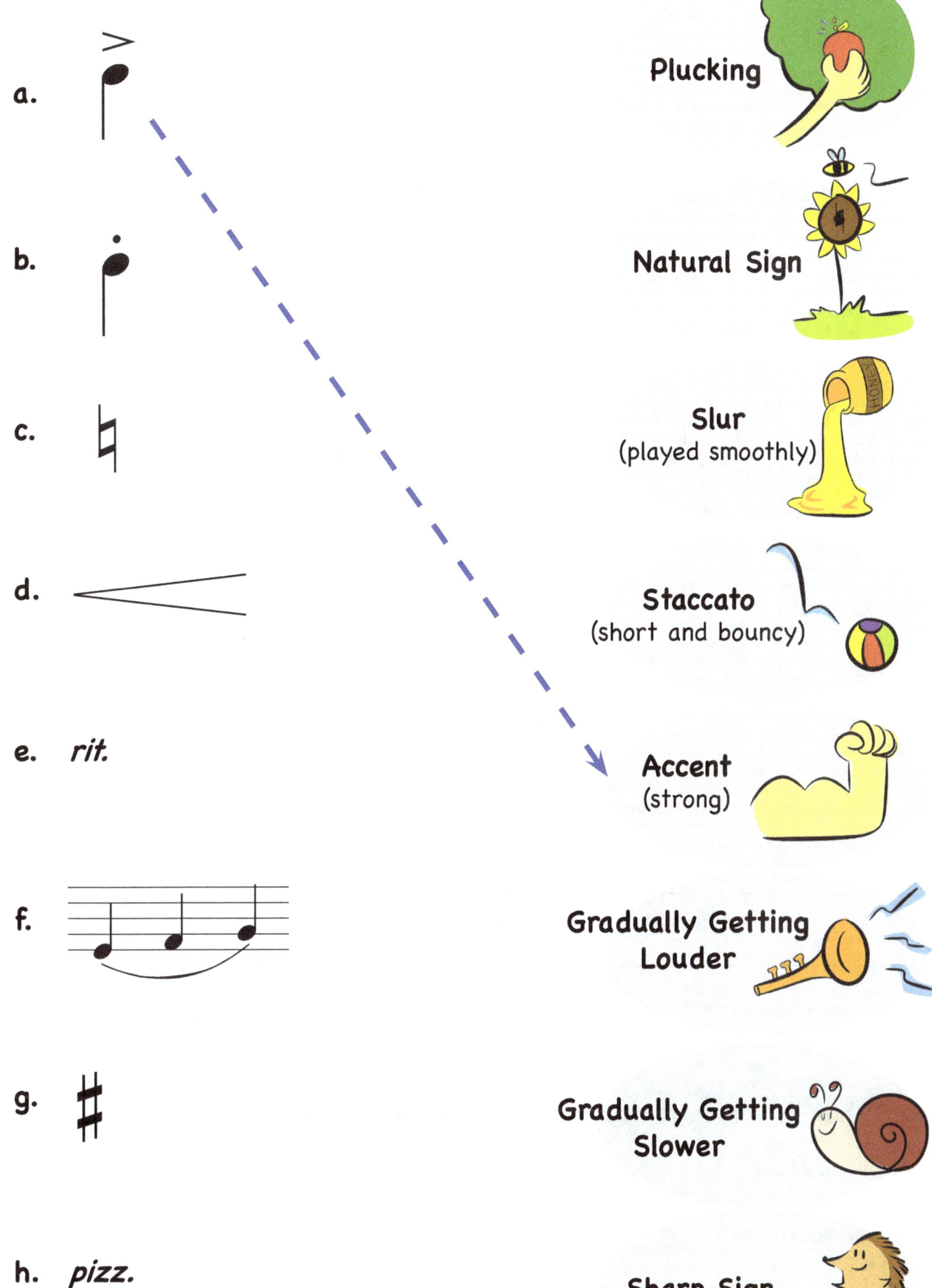

Last Revision

1. Name the string where each of these notes is from.
   (Careful of fingering.)

①②③	G	D String
①②③	F	
①②③	C	
①②③	C	
①②③	B♭	

①②③	A	
①②③	D	
①②③	E♭	
①②③	D	
①②③	F	

2. What is the difference between tempo and dynamics?

_____

_____

3. What do these tempo markings below mean?

   a. Moderato -

   b. Allegro -

   c. Andante -

4. Place the correct articulation/markings to these notes and explain their meaning.

MARKINGS	ARTICULATION	MEANING
Eg. (accent mark on note)	accent	*strong*
(three notes)	slur	
(two notes)	hooked notes	
(note)	sharp	
(note)	tenuto	
(note)	flat	
(note)	staccato	
(note)	natural	

46

5. What is the difference between key signature and accidental?

_____

_____

6. Write out these scales using the correct key signature.
(Remember to draw the alto clef.)

D major
- One octave ascending only
- Use semibreve notes
- Complete the scale with a double bar line

C major
- One octave in an ascending and descending order
- Use semibreve notes
- Complete the scale with a double bar line

7. Write out these scales using the correct accidentals.

G major
- One octave descending only
- Use semibreve notes
- Complete the scale with a double bar line

8. Write out the appropriate fingering for questions 6 and 7 and play them.

www.stringstastic.com

Name: _____ Date: _____

Test

TOTAL MARKS: _____ /100

Example 1

Example 2

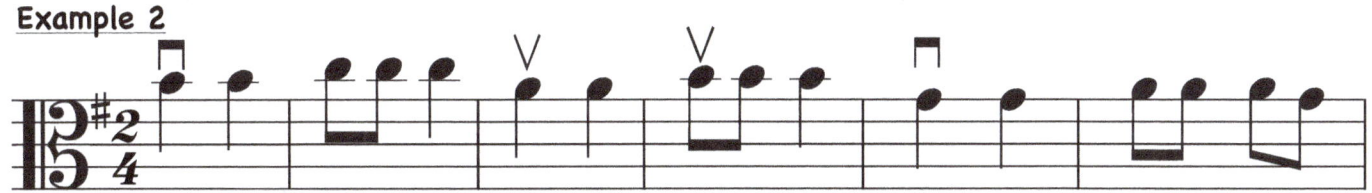

1. Put the number 4 (4th finger) on top of notes where you think they should be best used in both example shown above. _____ /5

2. Circle the notes where 2nd finger is used. _____ /8

3. Put an arrow (↓ , ↑) to show if the 2nd finger is placed next to the 1st finger or placed next to the 3rd finger. _____ /8

4. Draw and name the 3 notes in which you can use both the open string and 4th finger. _____ /12

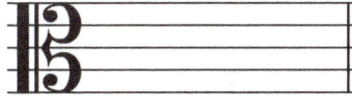 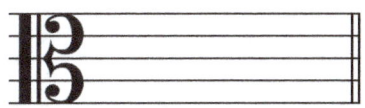

_____ _____ _____

48

5. Fill in the blanks. _____/10

TERMS	DYNAMICS / TEMPO	MEANING
Eg. p	Dynamics	Soft
allegro		
andante		
$<$		
accel.		
mf		

6. How many spoons full of sugar should go into each drink? _____/8

7. How many times does Suzie and her friends rest before they get home? _____/8

Robert the Chicken: _____

Cindy the Rabbit: _____

Max the Snake: _____

Suzie the Koala: _____

8. Fill in the blanks. _____/4

	NAME THE LINE UNDER THE NOTES	HOW DO YOU PLAY THESE NOTES?

9. **Write a D major scale:** _____/5
   - Start the scale with a alto clef
   - Use accidentals
   - Use minim notes
   - Write one on an ascending order
   - Complete the scale with a double bar line

10. **Now fill in the notes for the D major scale** (1 octave) **on the viola fingerboard.**

   _____/8

   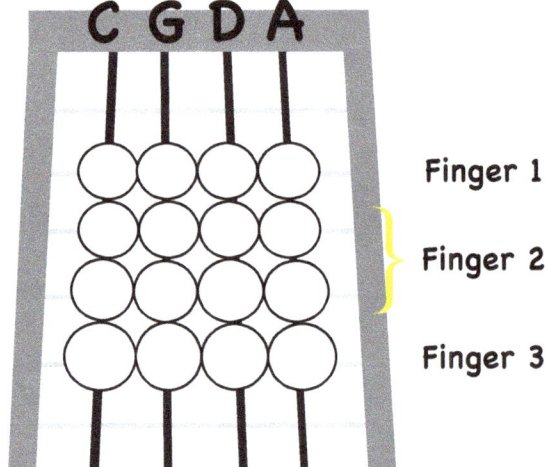

11. **There are 4 mistakes in the following G major scale. Circle them and rewrite the correct scale.** _____/14

12. Where would you be able to add a tied in the tune below?

___/2

13. Name these signs and its definition. ___/8

a.  -

b.  -

c.  -

d. 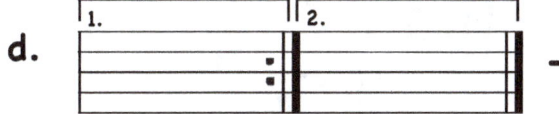 -

e. *rit.* -

f. *dolce* -

g. *Da Capo (D.C.)* -

h. *Fine* -

www.ingramcontent.com/pod-product-compliance
Lightning Source LLC
Chambersburg PA
CBHW080857010526
44107CB00058B/2606